The Picture History of
The Somerset &
Dorset Railway

Near Midford about 1925: a down express conveying Midland coaches from the North on Tucking Mill viaduct with rebuilt Johnson 4-4-0 No 70 (from a painting by Victor Welch)

The Picture History of The Somerset & Dorset Railway

Robin Atthill

DAVID & CHARLES

NEWTON ABBOT   LONDON   NORTH POMFRET (Vt)

By the same author

THE SOMERSET & DORSET RAILWAY

ISBN: 978-1-4463-0651-2

© Robin Atthill and Ivo Peters 1970

First published 1970
Second impression 1980

Printed in Great Britain
by Redwood Burn Ltd Trowbridge & Esher
for David & Charles (Publishers) Limited
Brunel House   Newton Abbot   Devon

Contents

Introduction

Mention of the Somerset & Dorset is still liable to evoke strong emotions—whether of affection or derision. In an era of standardisation and conformity it retained to the end an intensely individual persona, deriving doubtless from its peculiarities as a Joint line with a chequered and absorbingly interesting past. Its closure under the Beeching plan caused more outcry and heartburning than practically any other closure.

Its attraction and charm was in part at least photogenic: its tunnels and viaducts; its fierce gradients and curvature; the variety and beauty of the countryside which it threaded, from lush elm-studded valleys to the windswept Mendip ridge or the sweeping outlines of the Dorset downs; chalk, heathland, limestone and mysterious peat moors with their deep-cut rhines. Add to this a number of operational idiosyncrasies, a fair proportion of vintage steam engines, and the marked seasonal variations of traffic—all in all it is easy to see its attraction for the photographer.

And the S & D was fortunate in its photographers. At the turn of the century Dr T. F. Budden did duty as locum at Blandford on several occasions and unforgettably captured the atmosphere of the line in its late Victorian heyday. (Having deposited the doctor and his cumbersome apparatus by the lineside, the groom would then lead away the pony and trap to a safe distance.) Between the wars H. C. Casserley visited the line just before the takeover of 1930, and W. Vaughan Jenkins lived and worked on it. In the post-war years many of the leading railway photographers found their way there, especially on summer Saturdays. Without their interest and co-operation I could not have compiled this book. In particular Ivo Peters, who has allowed me to choose freely from his unique collection while himself making his own selection in one of the later chapters.

I have attempted to tell the whole story of the S & D in pictures from 1854 to 1966. In a sense this book is complementary to my history *The Somerset & Dorset Railway* and I have not reproduced any photographs from that volume. I have searched far and wide, and boxrooms and family albums have yielded their quota of rare and fascinating historical pictures. I am well aware that there are gaps in the record: before 1914, for instance, photographs of scenes north of Evercreech are very rare; some aspects of the line seem never to have been photographed at all; certain other pictures have tantalisingly eluded me though I have reason to know that they exist. Every reader will decry some particular omission. But I am quite unrepentant because this is a personal picture history, and I dedicate it gratefully to all those who built and worked and loved the S & D.

Ashwick, Oakhill,

Charlton Marshall 1900-60: Dr Budden's picture of a down Bournemouth train behind 4-4-0 No 15 contrasted with Ivo Peters' picture of 2-10-0 No 92203. Apart from the derelict platform of Charlton Marshall Halt, the setting with its trees and its graceful red-brick arch has not changed—nor has the S & D passenger head-code.

Independent Days

The Somerset & Dorset Railway was born on 1 September 1862 of the union of the Somerset Central and the Dorset Central. The Somerset Central—a 12-mile broad-gauge line from Highbridge to Glastonbury, worked by the Bristol & Exeter—was opened for regular traffic on 28 August 1854. Its centenary was commemorated by a special train from Glastonbury to Burnham on 28 August 1954. James Clark of Street had been one of the chief promoters of the SCR and the celebration was organised by C. & J. Clark and Clark, Son & Morland, the two firms in which he had been a first partner. Descendants of James Clark and employees of the two firms, with their families, many of them in period costume, filled the twelve-coach train which was hauled by a Johnson 3F 0-6-0, formerly SDJR No 64.

The SCR was extended to Burnham and Wells in 1858 and 1859; the narrow-gauge DCR was opened from Wimborne to Blandford in 1860; and a link-up at Cole was planned, in preparation for which a third rail was laid on the SCR. Amalgamation followed, and in 1863 through working was begun over 60 miles of line from Burnham to Wimborne (with running powers into Poole over the LSWR) with the Somerset & Dorset's own narrow-gauge stock. *(Above)* No 9, a George England 2-4-0 acquired in 1863. *(Below)* Another England 2-4-0 design, nicknamed 'Bluebottle', worked on the Glastonbury—Wells branch 1863-70. The figure on the left has been identified as Robert Read, Secretary and General Manager of of the S & D until 1891. Both engines carried jacks on the running plate.

The Joint Line before 1914

In 1874 the extension from Evercreech to join the Midland Railway at Bath was opened, and through running was achieved over the new main line from Bath to Bournemouth, which was reached over the LSWR from Wimborne. Financial difficulties however led to the lease of the line jointly to the MR and LSWR from 1 November 1875. The task of re-organisation and consolidation fell chiefly upon Robert Dykes, the first Traffic Superintendent (1876-1902). In 1899 Dykes wrote, 'By dint of unceasing labour . . . we have succeeded in placing our line on a par with any in the kingdom', and on his retirement he paid tribute to the loyal service of his staff.

South Western and Midland Railway Companies'
SOMERSET AND DORSET JOINT LINE.

Bath, June 30th, 1902.

To the Staff of the

Somerset and Dorset Joint Line.

In retiring from the position of Traffic Superintendent of the Somerset and Dorset Joint Line, after holding the appointment for more than 25 years, and a total railway service of 52½ years, I cannot do so without a feeling of regret at the severance of ties that have so long continued between the Staff of the Line and myself, and I would desire most sincerely to thank one and all the members of the various departments for their much valued assistance accorded to me in carrying out the working of the railway, and to the Staff of the Traffic Department more immediately under my supervision, I would especially tender my thanks for the support they have afforded me, and the hearty way in which they have carried out their duties.

In conclusion I would desire to express my best wishes for the future as regards all my fellow servants of the Somerset Joint Committee, in whose welfare I need hardly say I shall continue to take a deep interest, more especially as I shall continue to reside in your midst and hope to be able to visit at times the various portions of the "Old Line."

I am, my dear friends,

Ever yours faithfully,

Robert A Dykes

The copy of Dykes' letter sent to Alfred Whitaker, his Locomotive Superintendent at Highbridge from 1889.

10

The crest of the Joint line combined the arms of Bath and the seal of Dorchester.

Stationmaster F. C. Bisgrove and his staff at Wincanton in 1883 with a Johnson 0-6-0 on an up goods. By now the main line was being doubled between Evercreech Junction and Templecombe. The station building with its characteristic awning, the goods shed and the signalbox remained unchanged until the end.

At Blandford c 1890, showing the S & D head-code for goods trains. The Vulcan 2-4-0 No 16A (originally No 20) was built in 1866 and scrapped in 1914. Here it does not seem to have acquired the full splendour of the famous blue livery.

A rare example of Dr Budden's photography on the northern half of the line: 0-4-4T No 29 climbs from Devonshire tunnel c 1900 with a medley of four-wheeled, six-wheeled and bogie stock.

At Corfe Mullen in 1912, 4-4-0 No 15 (now rebuilt by Deeley, see p7) takes the direct route to Broadstone opened in 1885; the line on the right is the old main line to Wimborne.

Pictures of the Wimborne section are hard to find. This shows Vulcan 2-4-0 No 15A on an up train of S & D stock near Merley between Wimborne and Corfe Mullen c 1912.

Engines

The first twenty engines belonging to the Somerset & Dorset Railway were all 2-4-0s including two tank engines: all these were built by George England except for the two Vulcans shown on pages 12 and 14. When the Bath Extension was opened in 1874, nine Fox, Walker 0-6-0 saddle tanks were acquired, and six 0-6-0 tender engines from Fowler of Leeds. Thereafter, under the Joint Committee, locomotive policy was dictated by Derby, and most SDJR classes were either variants on standard Midland types designed specially for the peculiar requirements of the Joint line, or actual Midland or LMS designs by Johnson or Fowler, though many of them were built by outside firms. The only exceptions were the three little Radstock shunters and the Sentinels which succeeded them, and the famous 2-8-0s.

'Up the bank': Fox, Walker saddle tank No 3 at Midsomer Norton in 1903 with shunter Fussell, fireman Brooks and driver Emery. Introduced in 1874 for main line work, this class survived as banking engines stationed at Radstock until 1930-4.

Driver Kennersley and his son on the footplate of Johnson 0-4-4T No 32 beside the Bridgwater turntable in 1905. Built by Avonside in 1877, No 32 outlived the rest of its class and survived until 1946 as LMS No 1230.

The Derby-built Johnson 4-4-0s were introduced in 1891 to replace the 0-4-4Ts which had handled the main line expresses since 1877. No 16 as originally built—a very beautiful design—standing on an up train at Evercreech Junction about 1900.

The S & D had a passion for renumbering. The original No 45 was an England 2-4-0 (formerly No 17); there was a colliery shunter No 45A; the Johnson 4-4-0 (*above*) eventually became No 18 to make way for a new standard LMS 2P in 1928 (*below*). Here seen taking water at Branksome, this engine spent its whole life on the Joint line until withdrawn in 1962 as BR 40634.

The Fowler and Johnson 0-6-0s bore the brunt of the freight working over the main line from 1874 until 1914. The Fowlers lasted until 1928; some of the class 1F Johnsons, including No 47, survived until 1932-3. (*Above*) Fowler No 19, rebuilt with Stirling type cab, on the Wimborne turntable in 1904.

(*Below*) Johnson No 47 at Bath c 1925 with fireman Beale. Donald Beale joined the railway in 1919 and retired in 1966. He was passed for driving in 1936 and between 1946 and 1962 he rapidly became one of the leading drivers at Branksome shed. (See page 60 below and page 7 below where he is seen on location.)

The Johnson 0-6-0s were known as Scotties because the first batch were built by Neilson of Glasgow; the later class 3Fs (Nos 62-66, 72-76) were nicknamed Bulldogs; all Midland or LMS 4Fs were indiscriminately known as Armstrongs because the SDJR batch were built by Armstrong Whitworth. Nos 57-61 left Newcastle together in 1922 and spent their whole life on the S & D, the class becoming extinct in 1965.

The 2-8-0s were designed by Fowler for the Joint line in 1914 (see page 23). Nos 80-85 were built at Derby and a further batch Nos 86-90 by Robert Stephenson & Co in 1925. No 86 figured in the Railway Centenary Exhibition at Darlington in July 1925, carrying on her running plate a model of **Locomotion** No 1, built by Stephenson for another S & DR in 1825.

Between 1882 and 1929 three diminutive tank engines, constructed or reconstructed at Highbridge, worked on the colliery sidings at Radstock, their dimensions being limited by an abnormally low overbridge (see page 80). Known affectionately as the Dazzlers, Nos 25A, 26A and 45A were replaced in 1929 by two Sentinel 0-4-0s *(below)* Nos 101 and 102, which survived until 1959 and 1961 as BR Nos 47190 and 47191.

Main Line 1914-1939

The S & D was not immediately affected by the Grouping of 1923, but in 1930 the LMS took over the operation of the line, absorbed the locomotive stock and divided the rolling stock with the Southern, who took over the track and the signalling. Highbridge works closed, the blue livery disappeared and by 1934 nearly half the eighty S & D engines—most of them vintage types now 40 or 50 years old—were scrapped; others moved elsewhere on the LMS and were replaced by standard Midland or LMS types. The inter-war years were thus in a sense a period of transition.

At first it was a case of the mixture as before: rebuilt Johnson 4-4-0 No 18 on an up local at Radstock in 1920.

Main line freight was still worked by Scotties; (*above*) No 49 approaching Combe Down tunnel in 1920. But six 2-8-0s were already in service. No 80 was delivered in March 1914 and, fitted with an indicator shelter for a series of trial runs, is seen (*below*) about to pick up the tablet for the single-line section to Midford at Bath Single Line Junction, the S & D box which disappeared in 1924.

During the 1920s five halts were opened in an attempt to compete with local bus services. On 5 July 1928 the whole population of Stourpaine and Durweston greeted the first train to serve their villages—trains had been passing through since 1863. The clergy on the footplate prevent identification of the Johnson 0-4-4T.

Radstock 1929. *(Above)* an up express at Tyning bridge: 0-6-0 No 60 and 4-4-0 No 45 survived on the S & D as BR 44560 and 40634. *(Below)* a panorama of SDJR motive power against a background of Radstock shed, terraces of miners' houses, and colliery tips: 0-4-0ST No 26A, Jinty No 21 (later BR 47312), Sentinel No 101 and Fox, Walker 0-6-0ST No 9.

Disguised as LMS No 326, SDJR No 69 (later renumbered No 43) at Wyke Champflower on a down local with SR stock in 1936. No 69 was the first Somerset & Dorset engine which the author remembers seeing, one spring day in 1925, passing Binegar on a down express. It was built in 1903 and scrapped in 1956. Here it is seen between Evercreech Junction and Cole at the point of junction between the two parent systems of the Somerset & Dorset Railway, the Somerset Central and the Dorset Central, where a spur was built in the 1860s to allow exchange of traffic with the broad-gauge Wilts Somerset & Weymouth line.

Start of a new era: the first public appearance of a Black Stanier 4-6-0 on 2 May 1938 on the 10.20am Bath—Bournemouth, south of Midford. Although tests had been carried out with more powerful Midland 4-4-0s—both 990 class and compounds—the 2P 4-4-0s and the Armstrongs were still working the heaviest trains until 1938. After the strengthening of a number of bridges between Mangotsfield and Bath, Stanier mixed traffic 4-6-0s began to work through to Bournemouth. On 2 May the 'Pines' was hauled for the first time by No 5440 which was to spend most of its life on the S & D (see page 65).

Up the Branch

Once upon a time the Somerset & Dorset main line ran from Burnham to Wimborne, but in 1874 Burnham-Evercreech became The Branch. Passenger traffic was light apart from excursions to the seaside or occasions like Bridgwater Fair, but considerable freight traffic originated from Highbridge Wharf, and milk traffic from Bason Bridge. The easy gradients offered a pleasant stamping ground for elderly engines, and to the end it retained its aura as an outpost of Victorian civilisation—the quintessence of the English branch line. A sitting target for Dr Beeching.

Burnham station was opened on 3 May 1858 and remained unchanged except for the excursion platform on the left. Over the horizon the line originally extended down a 1 in 23 gradient on to the stone pier from which the S & D operated a spasmodic ferry service to Cardiff.

Wells (Priory Road) looking east. This was a terminus from 1859 until 1878 when the GWR linked its East Somerset line from Witham to its Cheddar Valley line from Yatton by running powers over 9 chains of the S & D. Until 1934 Great Western trains—one is here signalled from Shepton Mallet—passed slowly through without stopping, to the consternation of uninitiated passengers who wished to alight at Wells.

The Wells—Glastonbury push-and-pull train (here hauled by ex-MR 0-4-4T No 1346 approaching Wells in 1937) was an experience to be savoured, especially if—as was often the case—one was the only passenger.

A Scottie shunting at Glastonbury in November 1894 on the flooded moors. The late Roger Clark recalled a journey to Evercreech on which the train seemed to be steaming across a vast sea of water, and the swish from the wheels was like the sound made by a paddle steamer.

Another Scottie (SDJR No 47, see page 18) still at work in 1930 on a down goods at Glastonbury. The train is actually standing on the Wells branch line.

On the Bridgwater branch which was opened in 1890 as the Bridgwater Railway, but worked as a 7-mile extension of the S & D from Edington Junction.

(*Above*) Bawdrip Halt was opened in 1923. A pre-war branch line scene with Southern rolling-stock. (*Below*) a Joint line survival at Edington Junction in 1960. Like other railway outposts, the station received its supply of drinking water by rail.

SOMERSET & DORSET RAILWAY.

EXCURSION
TO
GLASTONBURY
AND
WELLS

ON MONDAY, 7TH AUGUST,
(BANK HOLIDAY,)
CHEAP EXCURSION TICKETS
PER
Special Train

WILL BE ISSUED AS FOLLOWS:

STATIONS.				TRAIN.	FARES TO GLASTONBURY AND WELLS AND BACK.	
					1st CLASS.	3rd CLASS.
				P M	**3 0**	**1 6**
BURNHAM	.	.	leave	12 40		
Highbridge	.	.	,,	12 50		
Bason Bridge	.	.	,,	12 55		
Edington	.	.	,,	1 5		
Shapwick	.	.	,,	1 10		
GLASTONBURY	.	. arr. about	1 25			
WELLS	.	.	,,	1 45		

The Return Trains will leave WELLS at 6.30 p.m., & GLASTONBURY at 6.50 & 9.0 p.m.

Children under Three Years of Age, Free; above Three and under Twelve, Half-fares.

☛ Passengers leaving the Train at any Intermediate Station when travelling with these Tickets, will be charged the full Ordinary Fare to that Station.

Offices, Glastonbury, July, 1876 No. 51 200.

A. DIFFORD,
SUPERINTENDENT.

GOODALL, Printer, Bookbinder, Bookseller, Stationer, &c., "Western Gazette" Branch Office, High Street, Glastonbury.

Excursions to the seaside at Burnham were popular from the earliest days: and not only to the seaside. This poster advertised one of the sixteen additional trains scheduled for August Bank Holiday 1876, that black Monday which culminated in the tragic collision at Radstock in which thirteen people died.

Blackpool excursion organised by the Bridgwater Allotments Association c 1910 with the help of station-master Hawkins on the right. Did driver Braund and No 51 get their tremendous load of eleven Midland clerestory coaches, including a diner, up the 1 in 72 to Cossington unassisted?

With an S & D pilotman on board, GWR Bulldog class 4-4-0 No 3367 **Evan Llewellyn** leaves Highbridge with a Weston-super-Mare—Bournemouth excursion c 1930.

This photograph of Highbridge station, reproduced from Alfred Whitaker's personal album, dates from c 1910. The original Somerset Central station building is on the left; a Johnson 0-4-4T heads a Burnham train of four and six-wheeled stock; in the background are the works (see opposite).

Highbridge Works

Thanks to the S & D the village of Highbridge became a sort of miniature Swindon. Opened in 1862 and closed in 1930, the works stood in meadowland on the banks of the river Brue. At best several hundred men were employed, and though no engines were actually built (except the three colliery shunters), full scale repairs and rebuildings were carried out as well as the construction of practically all the coaching stock and goods wagons belonging to the Joint line.

Another photograph from Whitaker's album shows a general view of the works. Looking east, the SCR line to Glastonbury curves away in the distance, the carriage and wagon shops are in the centre, and the erecting shop is in the background, right.

A complete set of photographs, taken shortly before the 1914-18 war, gives a wonderful picture of the different shops, their equipment and the range of work carried out there, as well as of the men themselves from foremen to apprentices. The photographs include the boiler shop, the general machine shop, the coppersmiths, the foundry, the general smiths and the spring smiths, the French polishers, the sawmill and the general stores. *(Above)* general view of the erecting shop.

In the carriage works. The coaching stock built at Highbridge comprised four-wheel and six-wheel vehicles as well as bogie coaches from 1898 onwards—all non-corridor stock. The photograph shows a bogie coach being built. Like the engines, the carriages were painted blue with gold lining. In 1930 the 177 S & D vehicles were divided between the LMS and the Southern and very quickly scrapped. Highbridge works have remained empty since 1930 except for the war years, but the carriage and wagon department was burned down in the 1950s.

A frequent shuttle service operated between Highbridge and Burnham, including a workmen's train which consisted of three vintage four-wheelers. A weekly season ticket cost sixpence (threepence for apprentices).

SDJR wagons: there was considerable traffic in rails from Highbridge Wharf. The Engineer's Department was based at Glastonbury, but rails also reached the LSWR and the SR from South Wales by this route.

Two of Alfred Whitaker's patent inventions: *(above)* the traverser in the erecting shop; *(right)* the tablet-exchanging apparatus introduced on the main line in 1904. (This photograph, taken about 1920, shows Bert Brewer, who in time became one of the best-known drivers on the S & D line, on the footplate of one of the Johnson 0-6-0s. See page 95.)

Shipping

Between 1858 and 1888 some sort of ferry service operated between Burnham and Cardiff, depending upon seasonal demands, Bristol Channel tides, and the economic climate. At different times the Somerset & Dorset (or its subsidiary, the Burnham Tidal Harbour Co) owned six steam packets and chartered others. But Burnham never developed as a port, and after 1888 only occasional pleasure steamers called at the pier.

Ruby, the first vessel of the S & D fleet and capable of making the passage to Cardiff in 1¼ hours, was stranded by the tide at Burnham and broke her back in 1863. 'Ruby accidents are among the ordinary topics of our seaside existence—they come as regularly as the tide,' observed the *Weston Mercury*. 'Should the **Ruby** again be put on the station in good repair, we shall anticipate in course of time another accident, while the infatuation of the shareholders attempts to sail her in a ditch'—a sarcastic reference to the inadequate anchorage provided by the S & D at Burnham pier.

Sherbro, a wood paddler of 239 tons gross, was by far the largest ship acquired by the S & D for the Cardiff ferry. Between 1884 and 1888 she carried cattle and market produce as well as passengers. *(Below)* **Sherbro** approaching Burnham pier.

Highbridge Wharf was a much better bet than Burnham and was used by private shipping until about 1950, though the S & D's own shipping interests had been wound up and their last two ships disposed of in 1934.

(Left) **Julia** (1873-1904), a wood ketch of 69 tons gross, off Burnham at the mouth of the river Parrett. (Below) the new **Julia** (1904-34), 197 tons gross, arriving at High-bridge on her maiden voyage.

General view of Highbridge Wharf in the 1920s; the second ship from the left is **Radstock,**
acquired by the S & D in 1925 and appropriately enough unloading coal.

Buildings and Landscape

Both on the main line and on the branches the traveller over the S & D was aware of the peculiar beauty and variety of the scenery. The railway blended with the landscape, but apart from the viaducts, eleven in all between Bath and Evercreech, the architectural features were relatively undistinguished. The line was built on a shoestring and the most important stations—Bath, Templecombe and Bournemouth West—did not belong to the S & D. On the Bath Extension there was a standard design for stations in plain grey limestone; south of Evercreech another—Dorset Central—design was repeated in either stone or brick.

Bath (Queen Square): the classical facade of the Midland station opened in 1870, four years before the arrival of the S & D.

Bath S & D engine shed, June 1958: the smaller Midland shed is behind the coaling stage and the span of the station roof is just visible beyond.

A down freight hauled by 7F 2-8-0 No 53808 (SDJR No 88) approaching the northern portal of Combe Down tunnel through the richly wooded Lyncombe Vale in April 1957.

The up platform at Binegar: a typical signalbox—local limestone, railway brick, wooden mouldings and finials. Michael Reakes was working the final shift on 5 March 1966.

Winsor Hill box glimpsed through the 132yd up line tunnel. Signal box and tunnel date from 1892 when the line was doubled.

Viaducts at Shepton Mallet: (*above*) Bath Road—the new viaduct under construction during the doubling of the line c 1890 (it was this new structure which collapsed in 1946); (*below*) Charlton, with an Armstrong (ex-SDJR No 59) approaching Shepton Mallet station with a down local in 1962.

Templecombe shed, as rebuilt in 1950, with a splendid array of motive power, smelling strongly of Derby except for a BR 4-6-0, an SR class G6 0-6-0T, and the station pilot, SR class Z 0-8-0T No 30954. In the foreground is the single line to Bournemouth; under the bridge on the left was the original spur to the Salisbury & Yeovil line by which trains reached Templecombe Upper—compare page 108: under the bridge on the right Templecombe Lower Platform is just visible. The roof of the station building of the original Dorset Central station is also just visible to the right of the engine shed. Opened in 1862, this remained in use until 1887, the approach to the station from the Bournemouth direction being controlled by Templecombe No 1 box which stood near the overbridge.

South of Templecombe, the Dorset Central line followed the valley of the Stour all the way down to Wimborne, crossing and recrossing the placid little river a number of times. Here a rebuilt Johnson 4-4-0 heads a northbound train, which includes four and six-wheeled rolling-stock, out of Sturminster Newton. The original Dorset Central line from Wimborne to Blandford was opened in 1860, the northern section from Templecombe to Cole in 1862, and the remaining 16 miles from Blandford to Templecombe in 1863 after amalgamation with the Somerset Central. It was a completely rural and scenically very beautiful stretch of line, continually winding and rising and falling along the hillsides or in the valley bottom, with the station buildings and the bridges all built of mellow red brick.

Spetisbury, south of Blandford, with its primitive station building. This photograph by Dr Budden c 1900 shows an old disc and crossbar signal still in use, and preparations for doubling the line through the chalk terrain. Almost inevitably a Johnson 0-4-4T appears at the head of a train of heterogeneous S & D stock.

POOLE RAILWAY STATION.

Industrial Somerset

One of the main objectives in the building of the Bath Extension was to tap the Somerset coalfield, and in the process the S & D bought up the tramroad which had carried much of the output of the Radstock collieries to the Somersetshire Coal Canal at Midford since 1815. Apart from the dozen or so collieries at work in North Somerset until after World War I, there was also considerable stone traffic from the Mendip limestone quarries which was handled at Moorewood, Binegar and Winsor Hill.

One of the Dazzlers, 0-4-0ST No 26A built at Highbridge, at work at Radstock sawmills c 1900 with driver Pitman.

Several narrow-gauge lines brought traffic on to the S & D. (*Above*) From Moorewood colliery in the Nettlebridge valley a 2ft gauge incline handed trucks over to little 0-6-0Ts which trundled them a mile or so to Moorewood sidings until 1932. *(Below)* Another little line linked Oakhill Brewery with Binegar station from 1904 till 1921. **Oakhill** and **Mendip** are here paraded with their trainload of Oakhill stout.

At Radstock the Dazzlers worked the standard gauge branch to Middle Pit and to the foot of the Clandown incline, and also the spur to Ludlow's. A mile nearer Bath, Writhlington signal box controlled the Braysdown sidings, which were served by an inclined plane, as well as the sidings which served the Writhlington pithead. Until about 1940 a 2ft 8½in gauge line ran parallel to the S & D along the valley from Foxcote colliery to Writhlington.

Gilbert Bray, Ted Lambert and driver George Swift posed beside their Hudswell Clarke saddle tank in 1912—a typical scene on the little colliery lines of North Somerset 50 years ago.

9F 2-10-0 No 92000 on a Bournemouth—Bristol train in August 1961, passing Writhlington signal box with the abandoned Braysdown sidings on the right. It was at this spot—near what was then known as Foxcote signal box, on the single-line section between Radstock and Wellow—that two trains met in a headlong collision late in the evening of August Bank Holiday 1876. Thirteen people were killed and thirty-four injured in the only major accident that ever occurred on the Somerset & Dorset.

Norton Hill colliery opened in 1899 and closed in 1966. **Lord Salisbury** (*above*), the Peckett 0-6-0ST belonging to the NCB, posed beside the bulk of an S & D 7F in 1963.

Coal shunt at Norton Hill 1960. On the footplate of Jinty No 47275 is shunter Lawrence Dando whose superlative gardening won many prizes for his station and gave untold pleasure to innumerable passengers on the railway.

People

One could fill a book with 'characters' from the S & D and the stories that are told about them. Some of them appear elsewhere in these pages 'on location'; this chapter comprises a cross-section of men who worked on the line—and some of their visitors.

Robert Arthur Read: Secretary of the SCR and the DCR; Secretary and General Manager of the S & DR; Secretary and General Manager to the Joint Committee 1853-91.

Alfred Whitaker: Resident Locomotive Superintendent at Highbridge 1889-1911. This photograph hung in the shedmaster's office at Bath.

Highbridge United: the combined GWR and SDJR station staffs (to say nothing of the horse) at Highbridge in 1900, under stationmasters Hargrave (GW) and Wilson (S & D).

Gilbert Ashill sets off with the Bridgwater parcels delivery in 1913.

The S & D at war: *(above)* King George V and Winston Churchill leaving Blandford station on 25 February 1915 to inspect the Royal Naval Division before it left Blandford Camp for the Dardanelles. *(Below)* In 1940 the S & D route offered easy access to the north in the event of Nazi invasion. A party of engineers is seen planning a defensive point at the river bridge near Stourpaine. In the background are motor trolley No 59 and W. E. Fox, Resident Engineer at Glastonbury 1917-30.

At Bath shed: Tom White (Running Shed and Mechanical Foreman) in working dress—he always wore a bowler hat—poses in front of one of his new Armstrongs c 1925.

Passed fireman Peter Smith, Locomotive Inspector Lawrence Whitley, driver Donald Beale and shedmaster Harold Morris, photographed by Ivo Peters before a footplate run on the down 'Pines', 31 July 1962.

Midford signalmen: Percy Savage and Harry Wiltshire, whose Joint service totalled more than 93 years.

The Pines

The 'Pines Express' was the pride and glory of the S & D. Unlike the other through expresses it ran all the year round, and its re-routing in 1962 via Oxford and Basingstoke was the real death-knell of the S & D—the end of through traffic from the North which the line had carried since 1874. 'The Pines' acquired its name in 1927, but the daily working of a through Manchester—Bournemouth West restaurant car express dated from 1 October 1910. Later, it included portions from Liverpool and Sheffield, the Sheffield portion running as a separate train at summer weekends.

1929: northbound, approaching Templecombe No 2 off the single-line section from Stalbridge, hauled by one of the new 2P 4-4-0s (Nos 44-6) introduced the previous year. The seven-coach train required piloting from Evercreech Junction.

(*Above*) 1929: northbound near Writhlington: LMS 4F No 4168 piloting SDJR 4-4-0 No 41—previously No 67, a 1921 rebuild of an 1895 engine which was not finally scrapped until 1953 as BR 40324. (*Below*) 1932: southbound at Midsomer Norton, one of the SDJR Armstrongs, No 58 (see page 60), works seven coaches unassisted up the 1 in 50 bank.

1938: on the footplate of one of the Black Fives approaching Wellow, piloted by a 2P. The identity of the engine and its driver cannot be established, but Stephen Townroe who took the photograph recalls that the Black Five was a 'foreigner' from Leeds, and that it was so rough that the brake handle was tied in the 'off' position with a piece of string to prevent it vibrating 'on'—which did not matter as the Five was doing the hard work and the pilot looked after the braking.

(*Above*) The classic partnership of 2P 4-4-0 and Black Stanier 4-6-0: Nos 40563 and 45440 sweeping south over Midford viaduct in September 1952. (*Below*) Two 4-6-0s: Black Stanier No 45440 and BR No 73051 northbound near Blandford on a gusty April morning in 1955. The BR class 5 4-6-0s had made their appearance on the line in the previous year.

West Country meeting point at Evercreech Junction: **Combe Martin** on the relief 'Pines' and **Woolacombe** on an up empty stock train in July 1959. Bulleid Pacifics first arrived on the Somerset & Dorset in 1951: **Crewkerne, Wilton, Dorchester, Combe Martin** and **Woolacombe** were allocated to Bath shed and quickly became part of the landscape, and many others of the same class worked up from Bournemouth over the years. Their nominal tractive effort should have given them the edge on the Black Fives, but because of their propensity to appalling fits of slipping, their load over Masbury summit was limited to 270 tons.

The BR 9F 2-10-0s appeared in 1960 and were allowed to take 410 tons unpiloted over Masbury—though assistance was taken from time to time. The up 'Pines' passing Masbury Halt in August 1961 with 'twelve on' at the end of the almost unbroken climb of 7¾ miles from Evercreech Junction, mostly at 1 in 50; 2P No 40697 piloting 9F No 92205 during the last month of service for the 4-4-0s, a type which had worked on the S & D since 1891.

8 September 1962—the last 'Pines', between Moorewood and Binegar, hauled by **Evening Star.** The load was 423 tons and the crew were driver Peter Smith and fireman Ronald Hyde of Branksome shed.

The Post-War Years:
Summer Service

Nationalisation brought new overlords and also brought a wider variety of locomotive types on to the line: Southern and Great Western as well as standard BR classes. Post-war summer weekends were fun, beginning in the early hours of Saturday morning, with continuous excitement to see which visitors would find their way on to the S & D, or what unusual combinations of engines the hard-pressed locomotive department would provide to handle the stream of holiday expresses. Towards the weekend an engine arriving at Bath from the North in particularly good nick would be conveniently 'forgotten', eventually arriving home with mysterious holes drilled in the side of the tender where the Whitaker tablet-exchanging apparatus had been fixed for an unscheduled trip to Bournemouth and back. Meanwhile the fraternity of train-spotters and photographers clustered at their chosen spots along the line.

Saturday evening: light engines returning to Templecombe after their stint of piloting. Ex-GW Collett 0-6-0 No 3219, 7F No 53810 and 2P No 40634 leaving Chilcompton tunnel.

(*Above*) For a brief period a batch of Ivatt 2-6-0s worked on the line without much success. No 43017 piloting 7F No 53804 brings an up express off the S & D line at Bath Junction. (*Below*) A pair of 0-6-0s passing Radstock in 1958: a Johnson 3F No 43216 (SDJR No 72), a rare visitor from the branch, piloting LMS 4F No 44422.

A Radstock Jinty No 47275 piloting 7F No 53801 on the 1 in 50 approach to Winsor Hill tunnel with an Exmouth—Cleethorpes train consisting of a very mixed rake of eleven coaches.

Maximum power: a unique combination of West Country Pacific and BR 9F 2-10-0 approaching Templecombe with a down express in August 1962.

1962: the last year of the summer service. A Bournemouth—Nottingham express on the beautiful eleven-arch Prestleigh viaduct between Evercreech New and Shepton Mallet. BR class 5 4-6-0 No 73049 and 4-6-2 No 34043 **Combe Martin.** Prestleigh was the first of ten viaducts to be crossed between Evercreech Junction and Bath—all originally built of grey mountain limestone, but some of them later rebuilt or repaired with railway brick (as shown in the frontispiece).

Dorset scenes: *(right)* No 34040 **Crewkerne** heads north up the Stour valley on the single-line section between Stourpaine and Shillingstone.

(Below) BR class 5 4-6-0 No 73087 **Linette** swings on to the S & D line at Broadstone with a Bournemouth—Derby train. The line from Wimborne in the foreground was the original Southampton & Dorchester route; the LSW line to Bournemouth was opened in 1872 and the SDJR cut-off from Corfe Mullen in 1885.

The author's son train-spotting at Moorewood.

(*Opposite*) Two BR 4-6-0s approaching Moorewood in 1960 with an excursion from Cheltenham Spa—class 4 No 75072 and class 5 No 73019.

Local Passenger

Impervious to seasonal ebb and flow of traffic, local services moved slowly—sometimes very slowly on schedules dating back to the last century—through Somerset and Dorset, or expired at Templecombe. Almost any class of engine might be observed on them.

BR class 5 4-6-0 No 73054 leaving Bournemouth West with the 3.40pm to Bristol—the up Mail which must connect with the 7.20pm Bristol—Newcastle at Mangotsfield.

(*Above*) Cole: a typical Dorset Central station with LSW type signalbox. Collett 0-6-0 No 3206 with a Highbridge—Templecombe train off the branch in June 1962.

(*Opposite*) Near Corfe Mullen, with the old Wimborne line on the left: LMS 4F No 44535 on an up local, coasting down the 1 in 80 from Broadstone.

The 3.30pm Bristol—Bournemouth (4.25pm ex-Bath) climbing the 1 in 50 between Mid-somer Norton and Chilcompton in July 1953 behind a 2P 4-4-0: these engines and their predecessors from Derby were the classic performers over the S & D from 1891 until 1962. This train was one of the semi-fasts, calling only at the more important stations. It was the return working of the 11.40am ex-Bournemouth West which between the wars had been a through train to the North with carriages for York, Bradford and Lincoln. Latterly it was cut back to Gloucester and finally to Bristol, and ran with a light load on almost the same schedule as the 'Pines'.

BR class 4 2-6-4Ts appeared late in 1963 and took over most of the local workings towards the end. No 80041 emerges from Combe Down tunnel with the 3.20pm Bath—Templecombe in October 1965.

Freight

Apart from an occasional 0-6-0 on pick-up goods, freight trains north of Templecombe were usually hauled by 2-8-0s. When the S & D 7Fs began to be withdrawn from 1959 onwards, they were replaced by Stanier 8Fs for the last few years before closure.

(Above) Ex-SDJR No 87 passing the former Radstock East box in 1960. The low arch on the right ('Marble Arch') once spanned the Somersetshire Coal Canal Tramway and dictated the dimensions of the colliery shunters, the only engines allowed through it.

An unusual apparition on a coal train: Black Stanier class 5 4-6-0 No 44841 passing Wellow in June 1962. This was a favourite spot for photographers; the beautiful village of Wellow, with stone tiles that seem to have strayed across the county boundary from the Cotswolds, lies picturesquely along the hillside, dominated by the magnificent fourteenth-century church.

(Opposite) No 48450 at Moorewood on a trial run in May 1961, photographed by Harold Morris, the Bath shedmaster, who was particularly interested in its performance.

One of the memorable sights on the S & D—a down freight approaching Masbury summit, 811ft above sea level, at the end of the 7½-mile climb from Radstock. The last of the 2-8-0s, SDJR No 90, banked by Jinty No 47544 in January 1950.

(*Above*) No 47544 watches the guard's van over the summit before returning to Binegar 'wrong road'.

(*Below*) Guard's eye view of fireman Eric Wilson on the Radstock banker easing off at the summit. (Note the tail-lamp already in position, and the uncoupling iron with which the guard had detached the banker as they passed Binegar.)

4F 0-6-0 (ex-SDJR No 60) on an engineer's ballast train at Evercreech Junction on a Sunday in September 1962.

The Branch

Parts of the Somerset & Dorset system had died before Dr Beeching swung his axe. The Wells branch was closed in 1951, and at the same time the Highbridge—Burnham passenger service was withdrawn although excursions worked through to Burnham until 1962. In 1952 the Bridgwater branch also lost its passenger service, though both here and on the Burnham section freight was handled until 1954 and 1963 respectively.

A nineteenth- or twentieth-century scene? A mixed train on the Bridgwater branch: 2.35pm from Edington Junction on Cossington bank in October 1951 hauled by ex-SDJR Bulldog No 73.

Another Bulldog No 76—LMS No 3260—also hauling a mixed train, collided with a narrow-gauge peat train on an unprotected level crossing near Ashcott on a foggy August morning in 1949. The 0-6-0 plunged into the South Drain, buried itself in the peat, and was eventually cut up and scrapped.

0-6-0s at work. (*Above*) No 43218 again, on a pick-up goods at Glastonbury, with driver 'Chummy' Andrews and guard Frank Padfield.

Another 3218, a GWR Collett 0-6-0 at Catcott Crossing near Edington Junction with the 4.0pm from Highbridge in October 1964. The South Drain formed part of the Glastonbury Canal (1833–54) on whose towing path the track of the Somerset Central was laid for much of its course.

Evercreech Junction—Highbridge train at Pylle, July 1963. Pylle station on the Bruton Extension was opened in 1862; a typical country station, built of grey limestone, rose-garden and all. The loop was removed in 1929; in 1957 it became an unstaffed halt and in due course nature took over. Ivatt 2-6-2Ts worked the branch in its last years. The bridge in the background (now demolished) carried the Fosse Way (A37).

GWR pannier tanks always managed to look utterly incongruous on the S & D with its affiliation to Derby. From 1960 onwards a few of the class were stationed at Bath and Templecombe and worked down the branch from Highbridge. Here No 4631 climbs through the woods that lined Pylle bank in June 1965.

Waiting for the staff at the former S & D Highbridge C box: a timeless scene with a Johnson 0-4-4T (BR No 58047 still in LMS livery: MR No 1303) on a train from Burnham in 1951. Highbridge Wharf sidings in the background.

The Johnson 0-4-4Ts had been introduced to work the main line in 1877: they could still be seen occasionally there in the pre-1939 era (see also page 101), but for decades they were the mainstay of the branch. One Sunday morning in August 1953 the Highbridge stud was paraded by driver Charlie King who posed with them for Ivo Peters' benefit.

Ivo Peters was the doyen of Somerset & Dorset photographers and assembled an un-rivalled pictorial record of the last twenty years of the line's history, comprising well over 3,000 photographs as well as film. His albums were passed from station to station down the line every year to the delight of all ranks of railwaymen. His car NHY 581—here seen at Chilcompton side by side with SDJR No 58 on a pick-up goods—was a well-known feature of the lineside scene. In the following chapter I invited Mr Peters to make his own selection of photographs to give a personal impression of the S & D as he knew it and portrayed it with the help of his camera and with the eye of an artist.

One Man's View

by Ivo Peters

From the summer's day in 1925, when I took my first Somerset & Dorset photograph at Bath, Queen Square Station, up to the last fateful Sunday in March 1966, I never ceased to be fascinated by the Somerset & Dorset. There were so many interesting and attractive sides to this railway—the constantly changing and wide variety of motive power used; the manner in which the challenge was met of having to operate one of the most difficult lines in Great Britain; the outstanding work of the incomparable S & D 7F 2-8-0s; the delightful scenery through which the line passed and, perhaps above all, the warmth and friendliness of the staff who worked the line.

Dear old S & D—the Serene and Delightful—what happiness and pleasure it brought me.

The scenery through which the line ran: The scenery throughout the whole length of the Somerset & Dorset was really delightful. Perhaps some of the best was just south of Bath where the line ran through the Midford Valley towards Wellow. In this view on 10 April 1954 the down 'Pines' drawn by 2P No 40634 (ex-S & DJR No 45) and SR Pacific No 34042 **Dorchester** has just emerged from Combe Down tunnel and is coasting downhill over Tucking Mill viaduct towards Midford.

(Opposite) A summer's day in 1925 and my first Somerset & Dorset photograph; a rebuilt Johnson 4-4-0 is about to leave Bath with a train for Bournemouth. Forty-one years and some 3,000 photographs later I was to take my last Somerset & Dorset picture.

The constantly changing variety of motive power: Horwich 'Crabs' were used extensively over the Somerset & Dorset up to 1949 when they were replaced by Ivatt's LMS 2-6-0s. Emerging from Chilcompton tunnel on 28 May 1949 is the relief to the down 'Pines Express' hauled by No 2897 with 0-6-0T No 7316 assisting from Radstock up to Binegar for the climb over the Mendips—driver Aubrey Pearce.

Other types might come and go, but for over 40 years the 2P 4-4-0 and 4F 0-6-0 were the backbone of the motive power used on the Somerset & Dorset. Running downhill from Winsor Hill tunnel on 5 August 1961 are 2P No 40634 (ex-S & DJR No 45) and 4F No 44422 with the 7am (SO) Cleethorpes to Exmouth.

The BR Standard 9F 2-10-0s proved to be excellent locomotives for the Somerset & Dorset and their use obviated the necessity for much double heading—but they arrived too late to save the line. Heading south past Shepton Montague on 21 July 1962 is No 92210 in charge of the 7.40am (SO) Bradford to Bournemouth with driver Albert Brewer and fireman Peter Smith.

SR 'WC' and 'BB' Pacifics worked regularly over the Somerset & Dorset from 1951 right up to the end of the line in 1966. They were not normally used in pairs however unless the up and down 'Pines Express' became unbalanced as used to happen sometimes at Easter and Whitsun. When the up 'Pines' ran as one train but the down was in two parts, two Pacifics would bring the up 'Pines' from Bournemouth to Bath in the morning and in the afternoon each would return to Bournemouth with a part of the down 'Pines'. No 34040 **Crewkerne** and No 34042 **Dorchester** are emerging from Devonshire tunnel, Bath, with the up 'Pines' on Easter Monday 1954.

Meeting the challenge: The narrow bore and unventilated tunnels. In the climb out of Bath the line passed through the ¼-mile long and very restricted bore of Devonshire tunnel; the gradient was 1 in 50 up and there were no ventilation shafts. As engines laboured up through the tunnel a great wave of heat, quickly rising in intensity, engulfed the footplate crews, and smoke and fumes would beat down into the cab from the roof of the tunnel less than 1ft above. Conditions on the footplate could be, and often were, extremely unpleasant. As S & D 7F 2-8-0 No 53809 came pounding slowly out of the tunnel with a heavy freight on 15 March 1952, the fireman leant out of the cab to draw in deep breaths of fresh air.

A spectacle which never ceased to enthral me was the assembly of pilot engines at Evercreech Junction on Saturday mornings in high summer to assist up expresses over the Mendips. From just after 10am engines would start arriving and lining up in the middle road. Some had worked down from Bath and, after turning on the turntable by the North Box, came backing down into the station. Others, coupled in twos and sometimes threes, arrived from Templecombe. Shortly before the first of the procession of up expresses arrived, five assistant engines would be ready, waiting buffer to buffer in the middle road. On 2 August 1958 the assistant engines were all 2P 4-4-0s Nos 40563, 40568, 40700, 40564 and 40697 *(opposite)*.

The long and severe gradients: The climb over the Mendips was a formidable task, with long unbroken stretches of 1 in 50, and called for enginemanship of a very high order. This was ably demonstrated on 2 August 1952 when, in the difficult conditions of a heavy drizzle, 2P 4-4-0 No 40505 and 7F 2-8-0 No 53804 in charge of the 12.25pm (SO) Bournemouth to Birmingham, came storming up past Prestleigh without any trace of slipping.

In all weathers: High Summer. 4 July 1953 was a glorious summer day—wonderful for railway photographers but stiflingly hot for footplate crews! As a pair of 4F 0-6-0s Nos 44557 (ex-S & DJR No 57) and No 44422 came pounding up to Chilcompton tunnel with the 10.36am (SO) Manchester to Bournemouth, the driver of the leading engine found it cooler outside the cab than inside.

Deep Winter: In January 1963 the west of England was hit by one of the worst blizzards for many years and heavy falls of snow continued throughout the month. Conditions on the Somerset & Dorset were appalling, particularly on top of the Mendips where the staff fought a losing battle to keep the line open and two trains were lost for some hours buried deep in snow drifts. Climbing away from Midford on 15 January is 7F 2-8-0 No 53808 with the 11.00am down goods from Bath.

The unusual and the unexpected: Only occasionally did one have the pleasure of seeing one of the graceful ex-L & SWR T9 4-4-0s on the Somerset & Dorset. The appearance of one at the head of a train usually indicated a locomotive failure at the Bournemouth end of the line, the T9 having been commandeered at short notice as a stand-in. On the evening of 2 February 1956 T9 No 30706 arrived at Bath with the 3.35pm from Bournemouth after the booked BR Standard Class 4 had failed at the last minute.

The Highbridge branch was one of the last happy hunting grounds of the Johnson 0-4-4Ts once so familiar throughout the Somerset & Dorset system; but after the 1939-45 war their appearance on the main line north of Evercreech Junction was very rare. During April 1955 however Bath shed became embarrassed by an acute shortage of motive power and arrangements were made to borrow 0-4-4T No 58072 from Highbridge. Her stay at Bath lasted a week and one of No 58072's regular turns was to work the 6.5pm to Binegar, in charge of which she is seen emerging from Chilcompton tunnel on 27 April.

The use of two Somerset & Dorset 7F 2-8-0s on one passenger train was a very rare occurrence—I saw this exciting spectacle only six times in forty years. On 18 July 1953 No 53808 (large boilered 1925 series) and No 53802 (1914 series) were making light work of the 1 in 50 gradient as they climbed towards Shepton Mallet with the 10.5am (SO) Bournemouth to Cleethorpes.

Farewell

Farewell specials ran over the Somerset & Dorset for some years, hauled if possible by one of the 7F 2-8-0s, for the line was 'an unconscionable time a-dying.' The last public service working of SDJR engines was on 6 June 1964. Old 87 piloted old 58 on the 8.15am ex-Bath, seen *(below)* climbing through Lyncombe Vale south of Devonshire tunnel in pouring rain.

Next day the same pair of engines worked a Home Counties Railway Society special over the whole system up to Bath where **Penrice Castle** waited to effect a Western Region take-over. *(Above)* Closure was eventually scheduled for 3 January 1966, but was postponed because of a procedural hitch. The S & D in fact died under an embarrassing glare of publicity which revealed the affection in which the line was held and the exasperation aroused by the handling of the closure. *(Below)* An LCGB special passing Henstridge on 1 January. This was one of the rare appearances on the line of a Merchant Navy Pacific —No 35011 **General Steam Navigation**.

2 January 1966. The RCTS had organised what was to have been 'the last train', here seen near Cole with SR U class 2-6-0 No 31639 piloting West Country No 34015 **Exmouth.** U and U1 2-6-0s had been tried out over the S & D in 1954 without much success. Thereafter they made occasional forays from Bournemouth in the event of the failure of a booked engine. At this point the special was about to cross the Great Western main line from Paddington to Penzance—a focal spot for train-spotters and photographers on summer Saturdays in far-off days of steam.

Four more specials over the weekend 5-6 March preluded the ultimate closure on 7 March 1966. Another LCGB special made a photographic stop at Chilcompton with Pacifics No 34006 **Bude** and 34057 **Biggin Hill.** This was apparently an unscheduled stop necessitating frantic telephone calls between the signalmen at Binegar and Midsomer Norton in an attempt to discover the whereabouts of a train that seemed to have disappeared in the middle of a 4½ mile section.

On the branch, the last public service train left Highbridge for Evercreech Junction at 4pm. (*Above*) Ivatt 2-6-2T No 41249 beside the Somerset Central station opened in 1862.

Overnight, after the passing of the last service train up the Bath Extension, the signal box at Evercreech Junction North was gutted by fire. *(Left)* A lineman up the telegraph pole was attempting to establish communications for the working of the last specials on Sunday 6 March.

The last train over the original section of the line arrives at Highbridge double-headed by Ivatt 2-6-2Ts Nos 41283 and 41249. The leading engine carries a wreath, but the S & D head-code has been removed for the next stage of the journey to Bristol over ex-GWR metals.

Templecombe Lower—the old Dorset Central station and the S & D engine shed with No 2 Junction box in the distance where the spur to the Upper station diverged from the Bournemouth line. A demolition train is on its way to the railhead near Sturminster Newton in June 1967 with NB type 2 No 6337 in whose cab the author made his last trip over the Somerset & Dorset.

Midsomer Norton station 1969. The station buildings and the adjoining woodland have now been taken over by the Somerset Education Committee in order to create a Field Study and Project Centre for practical work to be undertaken by local secondary schools.

The end of the line: Burnham pier.

Sources of Illustrations and Acknowledgements

I am grateful to the following for courteously allowing me to reproduce photographs in their possession or of which they hold the copyright. In one or two instances it has not proved possible to trace the holder of the copyright in spite of every effort; any such failure is purely unintentional and is much regretted.

The Rev J. Ainslie, 87 (above); J. Alsop, 51; Mrs B. M. Ashill, 58; Mrs F. Ashman, 52; author, 46 (above), 75; D. H. Ballantyne, 102, 105, 108 (above); Miss J. Bingham, 53 (above, below); J. W. Blanchard, 65 (below); A. E. Brewer, 39 (below); British Rail, 9 (above, below), 11 (above), 19, 21 (above), 32, 38 (above, below), 41 (above), 43, 44, 57 (below), 62; Mrs Bullock, 60 (above); H. C. Casserley, 21 (below), 25 (above, below), 29 (below), 63 (above, below); W. B. Champion, 36, 37; B. Chapman, 49; C. & J. Clark, 30 (above); Derek Cross, 47 (below), 55, 56 (below), 67, 69, 71 (above), 76 (above), 77, 81, 88, 89, 102, 103 (above, below), 107; D. Diment, 33 (above); J. Dyett, 18 (above); D. V. Emery, 15; Grahame Farr collection, 40; R. A. H. Hennessey, 109; Mrs D. Holley, 16 (above); H. G. W. Household collection, 23 (below); A. L. Kimber collection, 42 (below); J. Lakey, 24; H. M. Le Fleming collection, 14; W. N. Lockett, 51 (below), 56 (above), 68, 72, 74, 78, 79, 83 (below), 84, 85, 90 (above); Locomotive & General Photographs, 7 (above), 13 (above, below), 22, 23 (above), 26, 27, 28, 29 (above), 30 (below), 31 (above), 33 (below), 50, 86; K. F. Marchant, 108 (below); J. V. Maybery, 16 (above), 58 (above); D. Milton, 31 (below), 106 (above, below); H. Morris, 80 (below); W. W. Newman, 11 (below); Mrs A. O'Shea, 104; H. G. Owen collection, 41; (below); Miss A. V. Ozzard, 47 (above); Ivo Peters, 7 (below), 45 (above, below), 60 (below), 61, 65 (above), 70 (above), 73 (above, below), 82, 83 (above), 87 (below), 90 (below), 91, 92-101 inclusive; Miss M. Read, 57 (above); Real Photos Ltd, 17 (above, below), 18 (below), 20; R. C. Riley, 66, 71 (below), 80 (above); Mrs M. Robbins, 54; R. E. Toop, 70 (below); S. C. Townroe, 59 (below), 64, 76 (below); W. Vaughan Jenkins, 8, 12, 46 (below), 48; L. Wood, 59 (above); M. Wyatt, 10, 34, 35, 39 (above), 42 (above).

The frontispiece is reproduced from a painting by Victor Welch based on photographs by R. E. Toop and W. Vaughan Jenkins.

Index

Printed in the USA
CPSIA information can be obtained
at www.ICGtesting.com
JSHW052019140824
68134JS00027B/2547

9 781446 306512